LEAD BOLD
LEAD STRONG
LEAD WELL

9 Proven Leadership Secrets

Anyone Can Learn and Apply

By Mike T. Lightner

Chief Master Sergeant (Retired), US Air Force

Alaska

Printed in the United States of America

First Printing, 2016

ISBN-13: 978-1535461726
ISBN-10: 1535461721

Dare2Dream LD Productions
dare2dreamleadership@gmail.com

www.d2dleadership.com

CONTENTS

FOREWARD

Don't you just love the title of this book? Lead Bold - Lead Strong - Lead Well

It seems so intriguing and I know in many cases publishers try to find a catchy title to sell a book, always thinking "what sounds good that will sell the book."

In the publishing world, sadly, there is usually very little concern or consideration if the book has the depth and value to match that catchy title.

Well, with this book, I can say the book exceeds the catchy title and truly is an expression of what it takes to fully presence these levels of leadership in one's life.

We all know learning leadership skills are important for everyone no matter where they are on their journey, but who you learn these skills from matters just as much.

I can assure you, the title of this book has been lived by Mike Lightner and is alive in him. My favorite book says "by their fruits you'll know them."

I know when you read and apply the 9 leadership secrets in this book your life and the life of your team, will be enriched and fruitful.

Paul Martinelli,
President of The John Maxwell Team

My journey of leadership has followed many paths, but the paths that have meant the most are the ones where I have met someone who either challenged my thinking or inspired me by their actions. Mike Lightner is one of those rare individuals that has done both.

When I first met Mike he was a Chief Master Sergeant in the U.S. Air Force. His experience in leading trumped anything I ever did. At that time, he was overseeing the leadership and management of over five thousand people including Active Duty, Air National Guard, Reserves, and civilians. And, while those qualities intrigued me, it has been his desire for growth that perhaps connected us best.

Through my association with the John Maxwell Team, I have gotten to know Mike.

He is the kind of leader that can take it up a level and take you with him. He listens before he leads. And he can paint a picture that gives you greater insight and clarity.

Those same qualities are true of this book as well. I encourage you to dig into "Lead Bold - Lead Strong - Lead Well." It is an invaluable resource for any leader at any phase of his/her growth. Mike leads you on a path that will give you a new view, a new focus, and renewed courage. The nine leadership secrets that he reveals are game changers, and his story authenticates the secrets. He is someone who truly understands the service, sacrifice and dedication needed to be an effective leader.

One final thought, the Air Force has a motto, "Aim High!" As you turn each page, and explore each chapter I challenge you to Aim High. Arthur C. Clarke once wrote, "The limits of the possible can only be defined by going beyond them into the impossible." I encourage you to set a target that tests the limits of the possible. Let your actions resulting from this book prove to you just how high you can go and how far you can lead!

Yours in Leadership,

Paul Gustavson

Chief Technology Officer, SimVentions, Inc.

Founding Member of the John Maxwell Team

ACKNOWLEDGMENT

I dedicate this book to my Dad, Paul T. Lightner. He has always been someone I have looked up to and aspired to be like. Even in my young rebellious years, when we didn't have much to say to each other, I still worked hard to live up to his expectations and to make him proud of me. I always knew that if I could grow up to be like anyone, it would have to be him because if I could be like him, I would be successful regardless of what I was doing.

Growing up, I watched as my Dad went from running a very successful business to losing nearly everything and then taking just the few dollars we had left over and building another highly successful business from it. During my last visit with him, I asked him "Dad, how were you able to recover so quickly?" What he said will forever change my life. He said, "Son, it was easy. I simply believed that I couldn't fail...that I would be successful at whatever I did." It is in that spirit that I write this book and share my experiences with you.

INTRODUCTION

"The challenge of leadership is to be strong, but not rude; be kind, but not weak; be bold, but not bully; be thoughtful, but not lazy; be humble, but not timid; be proud, but not arrogant; have humor, but without folly."

– Jim Rohn

Do you believe leaders are born? In the early years of my career, I believed that I didn't stand a chance of ever becoming a successful leader. This was largely because I had developed a belief that leaders were born and not made. Perhaps many of you have heard or come to believe this as well. I'm here to tell you, after 30 years in the Air Force, I have learned that nothing is further from the truth. In this book I will share with you nine of the lessons I learned throughout my career. These lessons helped me to become a successful leader and I guarantee you, if you apply them, they will help you to become a successful leader too.

Before I get started, I think it's important that I share a little bit about my background. I was born in a small farm town in Northern Illinois called Belvidere. I was blessed with two wonderful parents, Paul and Joyce Lightner, and seven brothers and sisters. Now, being the youngest of eight kids growing up, my focus honestly was to get out of the house as quickly as I could. Because of this, my decision to enlist in the Air Force wasn't a surprise to anyone.

In fact, I had decided when I was ten years old I was going into the Air Force. My dream was to be a pilot. Not just any pilot, I was going to be a pilot in their premier aerial demonstration squadron, the Thunderbirds. Unfortunately, in Elementary School, I was told I had a reading disability and from that point on I believed that I simply wasn't smart enough to ever make this dream become a reality. So, at the age of 17, I settled for whatever the Air Force would give me. I enlisted in the United States Air Force in December of 1985 and in June of 1986, shortly after graduating high school, I was on my way to basic training.

Like a lot of Airmen in the early years of service, I struggled. Lucky for me, under the mentorship of my supervisor, Steve Nitahara, I was able to overcome many of these challenges. However, based on feedback I had received during my early school years, I never really expected to amount to anything. In fact, looking back there were probably many things I did to make sure that this image I had of myself remained true.

After three years of feeling like "I didn't fit in" and "this Air Force thing wasn't working out" I had made my decision not to reenlist. One night I was talking to my lifelong friend Scott Frazer about separating from the Air Force. As we talked about all the fun we were going to have when I got back home, he told me he had talked with his boss and he was going to set me up with a job. We were so excited. That was until later that night when I had a chance to sit down and think about what was about to happen. You see, I had been working on multi-million dollar aircraft and seeing parts of the world I had only dreamed of seeing. Now, I was about to give that up so that I could go back to Belvidere, Illinois, and deliver pizzas for a living...oh heck no! The next day, I went in and begged my boss to help me reenlist and I've never looked back.

Interestingly enough, with this new found realization came a new level of commitment which seemed to end many of my off duty troubles and my career seemed to really start to take off. In fact, within a year of reenlisting I was selected to serve as a member of the support team for the Thunderbirds, a position I proudly held for over four years.

As I started to climb through the ranks, I was fortunate enough to work in small squadrons which didn't require much leadership ability to keep them successful. That was of course until 1996 when I was put in charge of the 90th fighter squadron, Aircrew Life Support shop, at Elmendorf Air Force Base, Alaska. Although at the time there were only seven of us, this was to be the largest team I had led up to this point in my career. To say the first couple of years were rough would probably be a significant understatement. However, we all have to start somewhere and I certainly did the best I could with the limited leadership tools I had developed up until that point.

Looking back, I was definitely not the kind of leader I, or anyone else, would've enjoyed working for. I didn't have a family and I considered people who did as having some sort of unnecessary distractions from being able to perform their duties. In fact, it wasn't uncommon for us to be working 12 hours a day, and often six days a week. At the time, I didn't see anything wrong with that. That was until one day, during an inspection, one of the inspectors called me out on it. I'll never forget his words he said, "Mike, I get the impression that you're so far underwater that you can't see the light of day" and that hurt. At least at first, then after having some time to think about it I realized he was right.

As luck would have it, a few months later, I was selected to go to the Air Force's Noncommissioned Officers Academy to study and learn leadership development. For me, this was a big deal because this was going to be my first formal leadership development course since I had attended the Noncommissioned Officers Preparatory Course nearly ten years earlier. Going to this course, I didn't know what to expect but I did know that I had a lot to learn so I committed to putting all I could into it. During the first week, they had given us a book to read titled "*The One Minute Manager*" by Ken Blanchard. Now, you have to understand, I had issues reading that went all the way back to elementary school. But remember, I was hungry. I really needed to learn leadership. So that weekend, I took the book to a local coffee shop and sat down to give reading the book a try.

At this point in my life. I could have probably counted the number of books that I had actually read from cover to cover on one hand. However, there was something about "*The One Minute Manager*" that wouldn't allow me to put it down. And as I sat there in the coffee shop, reading it and drinking coffee, before I knew it, I had read the entire thing. In fact, there were several pages that I had marked with scraps of napkins that I went back and studied again before I left. I can't explain what was going on or why but, for the first time in my life, I was actually excited about learning. For me, this was the start of what has now been a 17-year study on the concepts, principles, and application of leadership, as well as personal development. It was during this period, I discovered the belief that leaders are born is a myth. I discovered first hand, for

8

myself, that leadership can be learned and better yet...it can be taught.

To read or hear someone say "leaders are born is a myth" or "leadership can be learned and better yet...it can be taught" can almost seem too good to be true. But consider this: I went from nearly failing out of high school, struggling as a mid-level supervisor, to earning the highest command-level team award in my career field, not once but four times at four different bases. I ended up being promoted to the highest enlisted rank in the Air Force and in 2012, I was selected to run my entire career field. I had 5,200 full-time employees stationed at locations all around the world. My income had skyrocketed, I went to college and graduated in the top 1% of my class. The truth of the matter is, I had always had the potential to learn, lead, and manage. I just lacked the belief in myself and the knowledge and understanding of a few basic leadership skills.

These leadership skills are something you can learn too. Perhaps the best part is that you don't need to go through 30 years of military service to learn them, understand them, and apply them in your organization. I have gathered them for you right here in this book.

Throughout this book, I will be sharing with you many stories from different periods of my military career. I share these not to impress you but to impress upon you the impact these basic leadership skills have had on my career and to help illustrate how you may see them materialize in your own organization. Do not let the simplicity of these skills deter you from using them. Often times, it is the simplest of actions which can yield the greatest benefits and that is certainly the case here.

PART 1

LEAD BOLD

"A good leader is a person who takes a little more than his share of the blame and a little less than his share of the credit."

~ John Maxwell

LEAD BOLD is all about taking initiative. Average people sit around and wait for people to tell them what to learn, where to go, and what to do but great leaders seek out knowledge, take responsibility, and create opportunities. Every person can take the initiative and learn to LEAD BOLD by making three critical decisions. In this section, we will examine each of these choices.

CHAPTER 1

STEP UP

Volunteer to help with projects; don't
wait for the projects to be given to you.

*"Successful leaders see the opportunities
in every difficulty rather than the difficulty
in every opportunity."*

~ Reed Markham

It doesn't matter what line of work you are in or
the organization you belong to, there are
always projects which need to be done. As a

leader, it is important that you volunteer to help with these types of projects and not wait for them to be given to you. Helping to solve problems and tackle issues not only helps your organization, it also helps to develop your experience, prepares you for future roles and can even help you earn some recognition. In the early days of my career, I can't tell you how many times opportunities would present themselves, only for me to "duck & cover" and try to figure out ways to get out of doing them. Sadly, I was the king of excuses and could talk myself out of just about any project. Perhaps you know someone like this or you're one of those people as well.

Lucky for me, there came a point in my career where I wanted to receive some recognition. After all, who doesn't like to win? Problem was, I hadn't really won anything before and didn't know what to do. So, I started taking a look at the people who were winning to see what they were doing. One of the things that I noticed was that when projects came up, before supervisors had even asked for volunteers they were stepping up and offering to help. Funny thing was, there was no shortage of people willing to label these folks as "kiss butts", "suck ups", or "bosses pet" yet I noticed that none of the people doing the labeling were winning any of the recognition. Clearly, there had to be a connection and I needed to give it a try.

My earlier attempts at stepping up came when they were looking for an Aircrew Life Support person to be part of the support team for a competition called William Tell. At the time, I had no idea what William Tell was or what I needed to do but I volunteered anyway. Come to find out, as a member of the support team my job was to get the aircrew life support equipment prepared for six aircrew members going to Florida to compete in a flying competition.

Because our organization still had its normal flying mission, much of the work that I was doing to support this team had to be done on my own time. Over the next couple of months, I worked hard building, cleaning, shining, and inspecting the aircrew's equipment, often times wondering if all this work was really worth it. Despite those thoughts, I had signed up to do a job, at this point I had no other option but to finish it.

Then came the trip to Florida and the competition. As I set up our aircrew's equipment in the aircrew life support shop, I began to realize something: all the other squadrons had mid-level Noncommissioned Officers maintaining their aircrew's flight equipment. In fact, when it came down to it, I was the youngest and most inexperienced person in the room. But I didn't let that deter me, I had a job to do. As far as I was concerned, I had all the skills needed to get it done.

When the competition was over, our aircrews had done fairly well and our home unit was very happy with our performance. Because of this, our team commander recommended me for an Air Force Achievement Medal and I finally got my first taste of how real recognition felt. And I have to tell you... I liked it! As it turns out, even though that recognition felt nice, the real benefit came a couple years later when I was selected to go work with the United States Air Force Thunderbirds. As a member of the Thunderbirds support team, I ended up using many of the techniques I had learned from the earlier William Tell competition to improve the support we were providing our aircrews. This is when I realized the long-term benefit of stepping up.

Are you stepping up?

Another example where stepping up had a significant impact on my career, which resulted in a positive impact for my organization came when I was a mid-level supervisor at Elmendorf Air Force Base, Alaska. One day while talking to the Pacific Air Forces, Major Command Functional Manager (the equivalent of a Regional Manager in the corporate sector), Chief Master Sergeant Chris Holt, he asked me if I could do him a favor.

Without giving it much thought, I responded "sure Chief what do you need." He went on to explain how the command needed a point of contact to provide support for the software we used for tracking all our aircrew life support equipment. The only details he had was that my name would be listed on a roster and if people needed help they would call me. If I could answer their question then great, if not, I was to call this other person to find a solution. It seemed simple enough and Command Program Manager sounded like a cool thing to have in my performance appraisal. So, I stepped up and took it on.

It didn't take long until the phone calls started to come in. It was at this point, I realized, I really didn't know all that much about the program for which I've signed up to provide support. The problem was, the person I was supposed to call if questions came up that I couldn't answer, didn't know much about the program either. So, I started to call other people on the list only to find out that half the phone numbers were wrong and for the other half, the people didn't know anything about the program either. Now, I was in a real pickle! I had signed up to do something I knew nothing about and the people who were supposed to help me couldn't actually help me.

What I did next surprised even me. I decided the only way that I was going to be able to fulfill my promise and provide the support that was needed, was to go to school. As it turned out, the program we were using was written in ©Microsoft Access. Luckily, I was able to find a school not far from the base where I could learn how to do programming and use ©Microsoft Access. After taking three different courses, the last of which, was a five-day class on building distributable programs, I finally had the skills I needed to do what was required. At the time, I had no idea just how important my getting this experience would be to the future of this program.

A few years later, the Air Force upgraded all its computers to ©Microsoft Office XP.

Unfortunately, this new version included an upgraded copy of ©Microsoft Access which conflicted with the program we were using. Because of this, when users tried to open the program it would crash and close. This meant there were aircrew life support shops all around the world which could not access the data on the equipment they were supporting. Fortunately, I was able to use the experience I had gained from those earlier classes to go through the program and correct all the code that was causing the issues. This not only earned me much recognition throughout the career field, it also saved our organization hundreds of thousands of dollars in man-hours from not having to re-collect all the data. It is this type of win-win STEP UP is all about.

I can't tell you how many times the knowledge I gained as a young mid-level supervisor has been used in solving issues and developing policy in my position as the Aircrew

Flight Equipment (formerly called Aircrew Life Support but the name was changed in 2008) Career Field Manager. Experience gained from working projects like manpower studies, Air Force policy rewrites, helping develop new data systems, etc., were reapplied in ways that saved time, money, and effort. In other cases, these experiences have helped me build networks of people, who have been instrumental in helping with solving issues outside my area of expertise. There is no doubt in my mind, learning to STEP UP has had a significant impact on my success and I'm confident it will have a positive impact on yours as well.

What have you done to help someone else or your organization that ended up helping you later?

CHAPTER 2

STEP OUT

Standup for what you believe is right.

"Leadership cannot just go along to get along. Leadership must meet the moral challenge of the day."

~ Jesse Jackson

There comes a time in all our careers where we have to stand up and do the right thing, even when it isn't the most popular thing to do. However, we must not let fear get in the way of doing the right thing. If it looks wrong or feels wrong…it's probably wrong. Be bold and raise your concerns. Don't just stand by and whisper "I told you so" in the background, stand up and say "I'm telling you" followed by what you believe the inevitable negative outcome will be. In the end, even if no one is listening, at least you will be able to sleep at night knowing you did what you could.

The first time I really experienced STEP OUT was during my first assignment in the Air Force. My supervisor, Staff Sergeant Brian Marang, had been told by our Aircrew Life Support Officer that the General wanted a modification done to a piece of his flight equipment. After researching the modification, Sergeant Marang had discovered what the General was asking for was not in accordance with the Technical Order. In fact, there was a warning in the Technical Order which stated that performing this modification could result in injury or death. After discovering this,

Sergeant Marang went back to the Aircrew Life Support Officer to tell him so he could relay the message to the General.

A short time later, the Aircrew Life Support Officer came back to the shop and told Sergeant Marang he had told the General but the General still wanted the modification done. The Life Support Officer then told Sergeant Marang, if he felt strongly about his objection he should go show the General the Technical Order and see if the General would change his mind. At this point, Sergeant Marang stepped out and stood up for what he believed was right. He picked up the Technical Order and headed off to find the General.

When Sergeant Marang found the General, he was standing at the Operations Desk which is where the pilots go to check the schedule for their flight times and other pertinent flight information. When Sergeant Marang approached the General, he started to show him the Technical Order and explained to him why he couldn't have the modification done. Out of seemingly nowhere, the General exploded, screaming things like "I don't care what the Technical Order says...I want the modification done" and a host of other more colorful comments which are not appropriate for a book such as this. In fact, the General was so loud, the Commander, Lieutenant Colonel Marty, came running from his office to see what was happening.

Upon his arrival, the Commander assured the General he would look into the issue and pulled Sergeant Marang into his office. After hearing the story, the Commander stepped out and agreed with Sergeant Marang. Believing what the General wanted was not a lawful order, the Commander forwarded the issue up to his boss to be addressed. Interestingly enough, the modification ended up getting done. However, the Commander met with all the other pilots and told them that none of them were to request the unauthorized modification. He then contacted Sergeant Marang and told him that since the modified equipment was no longer serviceable we had no responsibility for inspecting or maintaining it. Now THAT is leadership.

There are some who may read this story and purely focus on the seemingly negative consequences Sergeant Marang incurred for doing what he believed was right. However, as a young Airman watching this transpire, this has long stood out in my mind as a shining example of how a true leader should act. Sergeant Marang put the safety of his pilots and his responsibility as the section leader above his own personal desires for promotion and career progression. Unfortunately, our Aircrew Life Support Officer and our Commander's boss were not willing to make the same sacrifice and for me, their example has long served as an example of failed leadership. Fortunately, Sergeant Marang didn't let this incident get in the way of his career and he retired with full military honors many years later as Chief Master Sergeant just a few years ago.

How would you have reacted?

This next example of STEP OUT was discovered purely by accident. However, it provided a powerful lesson which has served me well over the years. A year or so later, after Sergeant Marang was moved to another section, his replacement wasn't scheduled to arrive for a few months. Because of this, I was put in charge until the replacement arrived. During this time frame, our organization was developing their annual budget and the Commander had asked me to put together one for our section. Having never developed a budget before, I really wasn't sure what it was he was looking for. So I went back to our section and did the best I could. I basically built a large spreadsheet which listed every part that we used and the quantity we used over a 30-day period. Then I multiplied that number times 12, under the assumption that doing this would come fairly close to our annual requirement.

After putting all this together I scheduled a meeting with the Commander. When it came time for the meeting, I nervously went in to deliver my budget proposal. Again, having never done this before I assumed he would look at the numbers and the data that I provided and simply approve it. Instead, he quickly looked at the proposal and then looked at me and said like "this looks fine. However, this year we have to cut the budget by 10% so I need you to go back and cut this down and bring it back to me." I'll admit, I really wasn't sure what he was asking me to do. After all, if I put 10% less gas in my car it would mean that I would be able to drive 10% less than I was able to when the car was full. This is simple math…right?

With shaky hands and a bewildered look on my face, I pulled out a copy of the pilot roster and said with a nervous quiver in my voice "sure sir, could you just tell me which 10% of the pilots you don't want to fly next year?" He looked me in the eyes and responded "what do you mean?" I went on to tell him how there was no fluff in this budget, I had use empirical data to calculate the exact amount of money that would be required to support the number of pilots we had assigned. The only way I could think of cutting 10% from the budget was to cut 10% of the pilots from the flying schedule. He looked at me frustrated and dismissed me from the office. I don't know what he was thinking and I'm not really sure it mattered. That year my section was the only section in the organization that was funded to 100% of their original budget, and at the time, that was all that mattered to me.

I'm not sure if my success in using this technique was the result of the naivety of my youth, or just simply dumb luck but the fact is the strategy worked and I learned from the experience. As it turned out, this became one of my favorite tools when it came time for negotiating for a budget. Had I not stepped out and stood up for what I believed in, I would have missed out.

Would something like this work for you?

CHAPTER 3

LEAN IN

Get involved and stay involved.

"Leaders must be close enough to relate to others, but far enough ahead to motivate them."

~ John C. Maxwell

Changes are happening every day and our people...your people...need you to keep pace. Sadly, this was one of those lessons I hadn't learned until the tail end of my career. Throughout much of my earlier years in the military, I considered the areas I was leading to be much like an island, somehow I believed my responsibility as the leader started and stopped at the door. That couldn't have been further from the truth. As the leader, your responsibility extends far beyond the shores of your island and well beyond the walls of your section or organization. You must look out far beyond the horizon and see what is there. Just as this will give you the time needed to warn your people of the coming storms, seeing what is going on throughout the rest of your organization will give you time to prepare your people for coming changes. Now, this example could apply at any level within an organization. After all, what good would an organization be, if the President or Senior Executives were not monitoring the market to ensure there was still a need for the products they were offering?

In recent years, I have had the pleasure of working with the John Maxwell Team as part of my personal development and growth journey. The John Maxwell Team is a group of elite coaches, teachers, speakers, and professionals, dedicated to using their professional leadership training, talents, and skills in the pursuit of adding value to people all over the world. Recently, the President of the John Maxwell Team and one of my personal mentors, Paul Martinelli, shared with me his views on the concept of LEAN IN and I wish to share them with you. I've changed these slightly to put my own personal spin on them but I believe they still capture the essence of what I had learned from Paul.

LEAN IN = Listen * Engage * Amplify * Navigate * Initiate * Now

LISTEN to the information being put out by your organization. Not only must you hear what is being said but you must listen with the intent of understanding. Regardless of your position in the organization, as a leader, you must listen to what is going on in the news, market, and feedback from your customers. Your organization is counting on you to steer the ship and you can't do that if you don't know what is going on around you.

ENGAGE with other leaders throughout your organization. Share what you have heard and listen to their interpretation of what they have heard. As a leader in the organization, you must engage with your suppliers, distributors, sales, and marketing teams. You must listen to their thoughts on what is going on and how it will directly or indirectly affect your organization.

AMPLIFY what you have learned throughout your area of responsibility. Use your knowledge and experience to educate your people on what is coming, how they can expect it will affect them, and what they can do to prepare for the future. As a leader in the organization, you must share what you know with other top leaders and work with them to develop a plan for getting the message out to the rest of the organization.

NAVIGATE through the available resources and use what you have learned to build a plan for the future. Help your people understand the coming changes in direction and the need for making adjustments to their current course. As a leader in the organization, you must make the required adjustments to the company's vision. This will help to reduce confusion, serve as an example of your commitment to the coming changes, and help to reshape your organizations purpose, core competencies, policies, and, ultimately, its culture.

INITIATE action on your plan. Managing change can be much like turning the steering wheel on a car. When driving, it is much easier to adjust the steering if the car is moving. Similarly, it is much easier to make adjustments to your plan once things are in motion. As a leader in the organization, you must recognize and reward those proactive leaders who are taking swift action to implement change. Similarly, you must identify and correct those who are falling behind.

NOW! Don't wait...get started NOW! Things will only get harder and more painful the longer you wait. You must ensure your people are on the leading edge of change or you run the risk of falling behind and playing catchup. As a leader in the organization, you must understand the price of waiting. Just take a look what happened in the world of photography. For decades, two companies dominated the market and were the world leaders in photography until they failed to react decisively and fell behind in the digital market. There are hundreds if not thousands, of other examples out there of companies who were the leaders in their industry, only to get passed by because their leadership failed to act.

Do you LEAN IN?

Although, in my opinion, the military has a long history of failing to LEAN IN and adapt to change during peace time, they have an equally long and distinguished record of adapting and overcoming to changes in combat. During my career, I personally witnessed many examples of this. One of the most memorable came during the buildup for the invasion of Iraq. At the time, I was stationed at the Joint Search and Rescue Center on an American base in Saudi Arabia. We had been operating from this base for over a decade in support of Operation Southern

Watch, an attempt to enforce the no fly zones in the Southern portion of Iraq. Based on information our leadership had been receiving and a shift in the political climate in the United States, our leadership determined a second war with Iraq was the most likely outcome. They took the information they had collected and consulted with our coalition partners in order to build a common understanding of how the battlefield was going to need to change.

Because of the unpopularity of the idea of a war with Iraq within Saudi Arabia, our leadership knew we would no longer be able to operate from our bases within the country. Because of this, they amplified this message to the other units operating within the country and began navigating their way through the options for new locations from which to operate. One of the final tasks I performed before leaving Saudi Arabia was to forward deploy to a neighboring country where we were in the final stages of setting up an alternate Joint Search and Rescue Center. In the event the war with Iraq was to start, all operations would be moved here and it would then become our primary operating location. Within a few months of my return to the states, my replacement told me they were, indeed, changing locations and within days of their move the war had begun.

Because our leadership had leaned in and prepared the battlefield, the forces who replaced us were able to decisively execute their mission without costly delays. I believe this proactive leadership not only aided in the swift execution of the war, in the end, it saved many American and coalition lives. Maybe you're not at a level where people's lives are at stake but you're likely at a level that could influence their livelihood. Think about it, how many people working in the photography industry lost their jobs when their leadership failed to LEAN IN?

As a leader, you must get out from behind the desk and find out what is going on in your organization and within your team. Figure out what changes are happening around you and how they will affect your people. Don't be lazy! Do your homework, then pass on what you have learned and make the needed adjustments to how you and your people will operate in the future.

How could you adopt LEAN IN where you work?

LEAD STRONG

"A true leader has the confidence to stand alone, the courage to make tough decisions, and the compassion to listen to the needs of others. He does not set out to be a leader, but becomes one by the equality of his actions and the integrity of his intent."

~ Douglas MacArthur

LEAD STRONG is about influence and there is no better way to increase influence than earning trust.   Sadly, many people will read something like LEAD STRONG and develop a mental image of a doctoral or controlling type of leader, when in reality LEAD STRONG is about humility, faith, and forgiveness.   In this section, we will examine three proven ways to LEAD STRONG and gain influence.

CHAPTER 4

TAKE A POSITION

For GOD's Sake...TAKE A POSITION!

"I cannot give you the formula for success, but I can give you the formula for failure, which is: Try to please everybody."

~ Herbert Swope

Regardless of the subject, there are few things more frustrating than following a leader who will not TAKE A POSITION and/or make a decision. Or worse yet, the leader who changes their position based on whatever direction the political wind is blowing. During my time in the military, I have had the honor of working for some great leaders who understood how critical their role was, as key decision maker, to the moral and welfare of the organization. Although I may not have always agreed with the decisions they made, I always respected the fact they had made one. However, like many aspects of being a leader, there is a catch. Once the leader has made the decision, they must be receptive to new information which could change the course of their decision.

This is probably best illustrated through an example which I personally had experienced. As the leader of the Aircrew Flight Equipment career field, one of my jobs was to ensure we were making the best use of the taxpayers' dollars. Shortly after taking my position at the Pentagon, I became aware of a number of positions we had which were coded as "jump" positions, meaning people were being paid monthly to jump out of perfectly good airplanes using parachutes. Because I didn't see a need for the number of jump positions we had, I sent out a notice to all the Major Command Functional Managers, requesting them to justify their jump positions or risk losing them. For those not familiar with the military, this would be the equivalent of a Senior Corporate Executive sending a notice to all their regional managers.

Once the deadline had come and passed, there were several positions we had identified as not having adequate justification to support. Of course, doing what we believed was right, we started the work of removing the jump code from those positions. As we were working through this, we received a call from the Air Force Academy. It would seem they were having trouble finding Aircrew Flight Equipment personnel with the right qualifications to fill their positions. As it turned out, for the person to meet their requirements for being an instructor, they had to have performed a large number of jumps. The only way for them to get these jumps was by being assigned to one of the jump coded positions we had in the field, positions like the ones we had just removed.

Now we were in a bit of a pickle (ok, I was in a pickle). We needed to make the best use of the taxpayers' money but we also need to make sure we were not allowing the mission at the Air Force Academy to suffer from our doing it. This was the perfect time for a second look at the program and the creation of a new action plan for how we were going to move forward. After reviewing the justification previously submitted by the Major Command Functional Managers, it was clear the positions we had removed were not in the right place to be jump qualified. We also noticed that the numbers in some of the Special Forces and Tactical units were not as high as they needed to be. When it was all said and done, we had actually increased the number of jump positons throughout the career field. This allowed us to meet the desires of the Major Commands and ensure the right number of folks were in the process of growing to meet the future demands of the Air Force Academy.

Consider for a moment how different this would have turned out if I hadn't been receptive to the idea my original decision could have been wrong or if I had stubbornly stuck to my position rather than admit I may have made a mistake. Chances are very good no one would have known for a few years until after I retired. However, when they found out, it would have been too late to correct the issue. The mission at the Air Force Academy would have suffered until they could get the required jump positons back on the books and the people qualified.

Given changes in your awareness, can you change your position on issues?

Another example of this happened back in the early 1990s. There was a big push by the Air Staff to push more decision making authority down to the Commanders in the field. To do this, they rewrote nearly all of the Air Force Regulations as Air Force Instructions and removed the term "compliance with this publication is mandatory" from the title page. Within months, everything seemed to be in chaos. It seemed like all the standardization in the Air Force went out the window and each unit was doing whatever the Commander thought was the best thing for their unit or worse yet, their personal career. This was especially troublesome for units deployed to a common location who were no longer configuring their equipment and operation the same way. In this case, Commanders were making decisions but they were not fully researching and following up on the decisions they were making.

Many of the functional communities raised concerns over the lack of standardization and the issues this was creating with training and equipping the people in their career fields. There were also concerns about the limited oversight ability of the Air Force Inspector General's Office and the functional communities. After all, if instructions are just guidelines and there were no rules, how do you grade someone on their compliance? Sadly, even though nearly everyone could see all of the issues, no one was willing to step forward, admit it wasn't working, and help chart a new direction. That is, of course, until a nuclear warhead ended up on the wrong airplane, going to the wrong base, without the proper clearance. Once this hit the national news, the proverbial cat was out of the bag and the Air Force had no choice but to change its direction. Sadly, it would have to do it with new leadership as the previous leadership was asked to retire.

As a leader, you absolutely have to be willing to TAKE A POSITION but you must also maintain the courage to change your position as the situation changes or new information is learned.   There have been many times throughout my career when I thought I was moving the ball in the right direction, only to find out later I was going the wrong way. Be sensitive to this and remain willing to plot a new course when needed.

How do you feel when your leadership won't take a position?

CHAPTER 5

DEFEND YOUR PEOPLE

Defend Your People But Don't Give Them A Pass.

"Leadership is solving problems. The day soldiers stop bringing you their problems is the day you have stopped leading them. They have either lost confidence that you can help or concluded you do not care. Either case is a failure of leadership."

~ Colin Powell

I can't tell you the number of times I messed this one up in the earlier part of my career. I didn't want to be the "bad guy" so I would either let someone else do my dirty work and discipline my people or worse yet, I would tell my leadership I would take care of the discipline and not follow through with it. In either case, I was failing in my role as the leader and it would take me several years and much frustration to figure this out. Reflecting back on my earlier career, I'm not sure why I didn't pick up on this lesson earlier. There were so many great examples of my previous supervisors' demonstrating this skill while dealing with me and my issues. Yet, the lesson seemed to have simply slipped by.

The first instance I seem to recall occurred when I was a fairly new Airman. For those of you not familiar with Air Force rank, the rank of Airman is the second lowest rank in the Air Force. I was in the shop helping a General

Officer put on his flight equipment. Because I was still in training, there was something that needed to be adjusted that I didn't know how to do. I looked over at our shop chief, Staff Sergeant Steve Nitahara, and said something like "Steve, can you give me a hand?" From the look in his eyes, I could tell I just screwed up royally but he hardly flinched and came over and helped me get the General out the door. After the General left, he called me in his office and proceeded to chew me out.

You see, I had called him by his first name in front of a General Officer and that could never happen again. This was nearly 30 years ago and I still remember his words nearly as well as if he was standing in front of me, chewing me out right now. He said, "Now Mike, you need to understand something about the military. We have our personal lives and we have our professional lives and the two must never meet. We can have a good time off duty and hang out and have some fun but the first time you bring that into the shop and it interferes with our ability to get the job done...it's over. We will only have a professional relationship from this point on. Do you understand?" I, of course, said yes and he responded "great than repeat what I just said" and, of course, I did. I have to say, from that point on, whether we were on or off duty, I never called him Steve again. At least, not until he had long been retired. There was no way I was ever going to make that mistake again.

Are you holding your people accountable?

The next example came many years later during my second assignment to Elmendorf Air Force Base, Alaska. I was a Master Sergeant, which in the Air Force is similar to lower-level executive position, working in the 3rd Operations Support Squadron. My supervisor was a Senior Master Sergeant and we didn't always agree on a lot of things. In fact, when it came to leadership styles, we were pretty much on the opposite ends of the spectrum. However, it was under his leadership that I would witness the single most memorable demonstration of "Defend Your People But Don't Give Them A Pass" in action.

One day, while sitting in my office, I received a phone call from a Major who worked at the squadron. Our Unit had just had an inspection and the Major was in charge of clearing up the inspection findings and documenting the corrective actions. There was one finding assigned to maintenance, but it was dealing with our aircrew life support equipment. The inspector had done this intentionally because maintenance had developed a checklist which required a specific action to occur out of sequence and she (the inspector) wanted the folks in maintenance to correct the issue. The folks in maintenance didn't want to accept responsibility for the finding and forwarded the finding over to the Major to have it cleared out by aircrew life support.

After explaining the situation to the Major, I told him that I didn't believe it was right for us to close out a finding that didn't belong to us and recommended he send the finding back to maintenance to have it cleared. He responded by saying "yeah, we're not going to do that. This is your guy's stuff, you need to close it out." Of course, that didn't sit well with me, so we went back and forth on this for what must have been a good ten minutes. Frustrated by the situation and the fact that the Major was clearly not understanding the intent of having the finding cleared by maintenance, I finally said "Sir, with all due respect, I'm not going to close out the finding" and then I hung up the phone. In retrospect, this was clearly not the brightest thing I had ever done. Without this mistake, I would have missed out on this priceless learning opportunity.

Within a few minutes of my hanging up the phone, I received a phone call from our Deputy of Operations ordering me to come see him immediately. The Deputy of Operations is the second highest position in the squadron and it was at this point I realized I was in trouble. On my way from the office, I stopped by my supervisor's desk to tell him what had happened and where I was going. Much to my surprise, he didn't seem phased by it at all. In fact, he grabbed his keys and said "let's go, I'll drive." On the way to the squadron there was an eerie silence, I had no idea what was about to happen but I was convinced my career was coming to an end.

As we walked towards the Deputy of Operations office, the Senior Master Sergeant looked at me and said "don't say a word, let me do the talking." As we entered the office, I could see the Deputy of Operations was clearly perturbed. As he started to speak, the Senior Master Sergeant was quick to respond and articulately explain why what the Major had done was inappropriate and wrong. To be completely honest, my mind was focused pretty much on the fact my career was over. I don't remember specifically all the words that were said. I do remember my supervisor going toe to toe with the Deputy of Operations in my defense. Of course, when the meeting was over and we got back to our office the Senior Master Sergeant proceeded to give me the butt chewing that I rightfully deserved. My career was saved but I still ended up having to clear out that finding anyway.

Interestingly enough, from that point on, I've had nothing but the greatest respect for that Senior Master Sergeant. Our leadership styles are still different and we don't agree on a lot of things but I will never forget him coming to my defense or the lesson I had learned from the experience.

You see, the Senior Master Sergeant knew something that I didn't fully understand. For people to gain real experience and learn they must be allowed to develop in an environment which accepts and even encourages them to make mistakes. As the leader, your people need to know you "got their back" or they will start to play it safe. It is the leader's job to defend his or her people from outside criticism, but hold them accountable when issues are brought to their attention. I only wish I had been aware of this earlier in my career, as I believe it would have made me a much better leader.

Do you defend your people?

CHAPTER 6

OWN IT!

No matter what IT is…if IT is your responsibility, make IT yours.

"What you do has far greater impact than what you say."

~ Stephen Covey

There are many reasons why I will never buy a rental car and nearly all of them are related to this lesson. After all, how many of you have ever washed, waxed, or even checked the oil in your rental car? I would imagine the answer to that question is probably pretty close to no one. Why is that do you suppose? I would argue it's because you don't OWN IT. When it comes to our own cars, we've all washed, waxed and even checked the oil in them. If we haven't done it ourselves, we've paid somebody else do it for us. Why? Because we OWN IT and most of us take care of what we own.

One of the earliest examples of owning it occurred when I was a young airmen. Our Shop Chief, Staff Sergeant Nitahara, was getting frustrated because our shop truck kept getting written up for discrepancies during inspections. In an attempt to correct the issue, he appointed an Airman First Class from our shop as the Vehicle Crew Chief and put his name on a placard where the front license plate would normally go. Within days, you could visibly see the difference this seemingly insignificant change had made. The shop truck had never been so shiny. Both inside and out, from the tires to the dashboard, the entire truck sparkled. In fact, I remember going by the shop one Saturday morning and finding this Airman First Class washing and shining the engine, which I of course thought was crazy. Clearly, he had stepped up to OWN IT and had taken personal responsibility for ensuring the truck was in perfect order.

What can you do to get your people to own their work?

A few years later, I was reassigned to Nellis Air Force Base, Nevada, to work with the United States Air Force Thunderbirds. After being there over a year, my coworker and I decided the shop didn't meet what we considered to be "the Thunderbird standard" and needed some upgrades. We decided to OWN IT. Because we were now in our second consecutive year of budget cuts, there was no money available for major building renovations. The only option we had available was something called "self-help." Basically, self-help meant the Air Force would provide some of the materials but all of the work had to be done by the people in the unit. Not allowing this minor (ok, major) issue to deter us, we set out and began the project.

The major areas of the shop needing to be upgraded were the cabinets and counter tops. Unfortunately, the self-help store didn't carry cabinets or countertops, but they did carry plywood. Not knowing what we were doing but knowing we needed to do something, we ordered a pallet of three-quarter inch cherry oak plywood and proceeded to learn how to make cabinets. I had no idea carpentry could be so much work and yet so rewarding. As it turned out, this project ended up taking a couple years for us to finish. But when it was done, those cabinets and countertops looked amazing and they really stood out. You see, not only did we make them with the utmost of care, when we were done, we had our painters put something like 17 coats (I don't remember exactly but it was a lot) of the shiniest clear coating they could find on them. I've been blessed and able to do some really cool things during my time in the military but transforming this shop was by far one of the most rewarding. It's all because we owned it.

How could you improve your work center?

Another example of owning it came many years later when I was a Senior Master Sergeant stationed at Travis Air Force Base, California. After only a few days at this new duty location, it was fairly clear that the training program, if they actually had one, was not working. Knowing full well that if the training program was bad, everything else would be bad as well, correcting this needed to be our number one priority. To get the process started I appointed a young Technical Sergeant to run our work center's training program. After sitting down and explaining to the Technical Sergeant what her responsibilities would be and providing her with some examples from my previous assignment, she quickly got to work. Within a few days, she had already developed a draft master training plan, reviewed everyone's training records and identified many of our critical training needs.

After seeing on paper just how broken our training program was, she realized there was little hope of our ever getting caught up during our normal work schedule. Because of this, she developed an innovative strategy for accomplishing additional training on Saturday. The goal of these training events was to address the training items which affected the highest number of people and would, therefore, yield the biggest return on our investment of time. Although some people were clearly not happy about doing training on Saturday, she didn't let that phase her and scheduled the first event.

The first event started out great. People showed up and knew exactly what they were there to be trained on. The instructors were ready and well-organized. That is, of course, until the building fire alarms went off and we had to evacuate the building. The Technical Sergeant wasn't going to let a little thing like that get in the way. She quickly adjusted the schedule to allow for earlier lunch. After lunch, we all got back to training, once the fire department had cleared us to go back into the building. Each time one of these Saturday training events occurred, she was there. As time went on, these events seemed to just get better and better.

Building on the success of the previous training events and wanting to give each of the sections time to clear out some of the training items which only affected a small number of people, she came up with a plan for doing a training surge two days a month. Because she owned it and took personal responsibility for developing and executing a plan to get our training program back in order, we were able to get back on a regular weekly training schedule within 6-months. And although this process started back in 2008, much of its original framework is still in place today.

No matter what IT is...if IT is your responsibility, make IT yours. Whether you're taking out trash, washing your unit's vehicle, or managing a team of 40 people, take care of IT like IT was your own. There are many reasons I'll never own a rental car, the largest has to do with how I drive them. There is no way I would ever drive my own car like that and that is because I OWN IT.

Will the work you're doing today make a difference three, five, or even ten years from now?

OWN IT!

PART 3

LEAD WELL

"People don't care how much you know until they know how much you care"

~ John C. Maxwell

LEAD WELL is all about people. It's the squishy stuff most leaders don't want or know how to deal with. I have found the saying "people don't care how much you know until they know how much you care" to be absolutely true and that is what LEAD WELL is all about. When it comes to words, it may not be as sexy as "BOLD" or "STRONG" but without learning to LEAD WELL, no leader or team will ever reach their highest potential. In this section we will look at three ways to LEAD WELL and make a difference in the lives of your people.

CHAPTER 7

GET INVOLVED

Leadership is about people...GET INVOLVED.

"Become the kind of leader that people would follow voluntarily; even if you had no title or position."

~ Brian Tracy

One of my earliest memories in the Air Force is a prime example of GET INVOLVED. I entered the Air Force in June 1986 and reported to my first duty station in October. In early

December, I received a phone call from my mother to tell me my grandfather, her father, was in the hospital and not expected to live. Unfortunately, my dad was out in Indiana with his parents who had medical conditions of their own. Because of this, my mom would need to fly to California to tend to my grandfather on her own. Remembering back to what I had learned in basic training, I told her that if she needed my help she would need to contact the Red Cross and they would contact my unit, doing this would allow my commander to authorize emergency leave. A few days later, on December 10th, the 1st Sergeant came into my work center to notify me that my grandfather had died and that my mother had requested my presence in California to be with her during the funeral.

He then calmly explained to me all the rules associated with the Air Force emergency leave program and told me how I could use emergency leave but the leave would be chargeable and I would have to pay for my own tickets. He then asked me if I had money to pay for the flight and money to spend while I was in California. Like most new Airmen I really didn't have any money, so I told him I couldn't afford the trip. He then said "the Air Force has programs that can help you with that, do you want to go?" By this point I was in tears, despite my best efforts to "man up" and hold it in, I did manage to squeeze out a "yes, but I really don't have the money." He patted me on the shoulder and said "there there, don't you worry about that, we will sort it out when you get back." He then walked over to my supervisor and instructed him to give me a ride home so that I could get ready for my trip.

A few hours later, the 1st Sergeant showed up at my door with some paperwork for me to sign along with orders, airline tickets and a check from the Air Force Aid Society for $500.

After signing the paperwork, he took me to the bank to cash the check and dropped me off at the airport. Within 24 hours of being notified that my grandfather had passed away, I was with my Mother and Grandmother in California helping to comfort them. I'm embarrassed to say, I don't even remember the 1st Sergeant's name but I will never forget the kindness he had shown me and I have spent the better part of the last 29 years of my career trying to live up to his example.

From my experience, the single greatest example of people who truly understands that leadership is about people, is the Men and Women who selflessly serve in the military as 1st Sergeants, Thank You!

Do you know your people and what is going on in their lives?

The next example of GET INVOLVED happened several years later during my second assignment to Elmendorf Air Force Base, Alaska. I was assigned to the 90th Fighter Squadron. We were about three days away from a short notice deployment to South Korea. Out of the blue, I received a call from the hospital informing me there were some issues discovered during my son's birth and his mother was not going to be allowed to have custody of him. After rushing off to the hospital to see what was going on, a social worker informed me that my son would be placed into a foster home until I could prove that I was a fit parent. After seeing my son, really for the first time, and still not fully understanding what was going on, I had no idea what to do. After all, I was a single guy with no other kids and three days away from deploying to another part of the world.

After returning to the squadron, I went straight to the Commander's office and asked him if he had a few minutes. Seeing what had to be a look of terror on my face, he pushed aside what he was working on and said "sure, what'cha got?" I spent the next 15 or 20 minutes going through the entire story with him. When I finished I finally said "Sir, I honestly don't know what to do." He thought for a minute or two and then said "well, the first thing you're not going to do is deploy with us. I don't want you to worry about a thing, we will find somebody to replace you." Next, he stated he wanted me to focus on getting and taking care of my son. He went on to say "I want you to go to the family support Center and see if there's anything they can do to help you. Then, I want you to go to family services to find out what you need to do to get custody of your son." He finished with "as a male I can't authorize you maternity leave, but what I can tell you is that for the next six weeks your responsibility is to take care of that baby." He stated he would be checking up on me and if he heard I was at work, he would have me arrested. Okay, in all fairness to my Commander, those last few words might not have been exactly what he said but that's what I heard.

Within a day or two of this happening, I was at home waiting anxiously to pick my son up from the foster home when there was a knock at my door. It was my Commander's wife. She had stopped by to drop off a basketful of things for the baby. Fortunately for me, there were things in there like onesies, spit rags, and formula I hadn't even considered purchasing. This care package was not only a lifesaver; it was a real eye-opener for the types of things I was going to need to take care of before I picked up my son. Again, a clear indicator my Commander understood leadership is about people.

What impact are you having in your people's lives?

Another great example which shows leadership is about people happened several years later while I was stationed at Travis Air Force Base, California. Like a lot of work centers with young men and women working together, some of them dated, and a few got married. We had a couple who unfortunately got in some trouble for what we believed was an adulterous relationship. In the civilian world this may not have been that big of a deal. In the military, this is against the Uniform Code of Military Justice. In other words, adultery is against the law in the military. After being served with a no contact order, the young couple decided to get together one last time before the young man deployed; unfortunately, they got caught and were both now pending legal action. The young man was allowed to deploy. However, shortly after he left, the young lady clearly felt she had gotten herself into a situation from which she would not be able to recover.

This young lady had a habit of doing things to get attention. So, when she sent her lover a message implying that she may kill herself it could have been easily overlooked. The young man chose to contact his supervisor, Technical Sergeant Robert McClary, to inform him of his concerns. Knowing leadership was about people, Technical Sergeant McClary swiftly decided to GET INVOLVED and attempted to contact the young lady several times by phone. Having no luck, he decided to drive to the young lady's residence to see if she was okay. After several attempts of banging on the door and not getting a response, he decided to break down the door to gain access to her room. When he entered he found her laying on the floor with an open bottle of pills and alcohol lying beside her. He quickly started to do what he could to wake the young lady up while directing for someone to dial 911 in order to get emergency services on their way. On the way to the hospital, the young lady died twice and was revived by the emergency medical technicians.

If Technical Sergeant McClary had simply blown off the young man's concerns as just another attempt for his girlfriend to get some attention or found some other convenient excuse for not responding, she would've surely died, alone in her room, on the floor where he had found her. It is clear, this young lady is alive today solely from the actions of Technical Sergeant McClary and his willingness to GET INVOLVED.

A large majority of leadership is about influence. Your position and rank will only get you so far, it will take influence to get you across the finish line. Get out from behind the desk and get out to where the people are. You will be amazed at the large impact a little bit of time can make.

Where can you make a difference?

GET INVOLVED

CHAPTER 8

PEOPLE MATTER

Every dollar counts but every person counts as well.

"Not everything that counts can be counted and not everything that can be counted counts."

~ Albert Einstein

Nearly my entire career in the military, we've been under some sort of budget cut or restricted spending. It started in 1991, with the "do more with less campaign" and is alive today in the form of "airmen powered by innovation." Now, I believe in the concept of spending limited resources more wisely. After all, what company or family in America isn't trying to get the best bang for their buck? However, where most organizations seem to go wrong, is they neglect to include the "P" factor in their analysis. The "P" factor is simply the people factor. This is the messy part of business and is hard to measure. So, most organizations tend to simply pretend it doesn't exist. The reality is that quality, well-educated, highly-trained, and mentally resilient people are expensive...expensive to recruit, train, and develop.

Inevitably, what seems to happen is that some "bean counter" plugs a bunch of numbers into a spread sheet and decides the organization can save a bunch of money if they simply cut or reduce the cost of training, healthcare, or any of the other programs related to the "P" factor. They don't do this out of malice or ill intent, they simply cannot easily measure the "P" factor's tangible return on the organization's investment. Because of this, they leave it out. What they and so many other people miss is a simple understanding of the true power of the "P" factor. It goes like this: A slimmed down organization with a highly trained, resilient workforce under well-developed leadership will always outperform a slimmed down organization with a poorly trained, unhealthy workforce under average leadership. It is critical for leadership to know about and understand the effect of the "P" factor. When budget reduction proposals come forward, they must ask questions like:

> ➤ How is this going to affect our people?
> ➤ Will it make our people better or worse off than they are today?
> ➤ How will it affect retention?

> ➤ **Can our people get treated better working somewhere else?**
>
> ➤ **What other options do we have?**

The reality is, most organizations have this entire process upside down. During times of financial hardship, they must be looking to invest more heavily in their current employees. This will enable each person to do more with fewer errors and less oversight. This can also help towards paying for itself by reducing the costs related to bringing on new hires. In the end, investing in the "P" factor can be a big win for the organization and for the people working there.

In my introduction, I shared my story about how I had gone ten years of my career with very little formal leadership training. The part of the story I left out was that this lack of leadership training was a result of those initial budget cuts in the early 90s. You see, some "bean counter" had figured out the Air Force could save a bunch of money by simply removing one of our four levels of professional military education, so they did. As a result, I, and other leaders like me, were left to fend for ourselves and figure it out on our own. I'm just glad my span of influence during that period was relatively small. Otherwise, I could only imagine the amount of damage I could have done. Luckily, about nine years ago the Air Force realized it had made a mistake and went back to a four level professional military education system. I only wish they would have brought back some of the technical training courses they had cut as well.

Regardless of the size of your organization, it is clear that every dollar counts. As leaders, we must remember every person counts as well... PEOPLE MATTER. There is no shortage of people in the world willing to provide statistics on how to save money but that savings must not ever come at the expense of the people. Too often we make decisions without fully considering the expectations and workload we are putting on our folks. Break the cycle, ask the questions, fully consider the "P" factor and remember: A slimmed down organization with a highly trained, resilient workforce under well-developed leadership will always outperform a slimmed down organization with a poorly trained, unhealthy workforce under average leadership.

Is your organization cutting the right things or the easy things?

CHAPTER 9

BE THE EXAMPLE!

What your people see is what they will believe is ok.

"A competent leader can get efficient service from poor troops, while on the contrary an incapable leader can demoralize the best of troops."

~ John J Pershing

Clearly, I have saved the best for last. If you learn nothing else from this book, be sure you understand and apply what you learn in these last few pages. Of all the things I have learned, BE THE EXAMPLE has by far yielded the greatest return for me both professionally and personally. Because I am very passionate about my work, I can tend to have a bit of a short fuse at times. Perhaps, you're like me. This has also been one of the most challenging things for me to master. Trust me, it is worth the effort.

We often question others thoughts and actions when, in reality, it is our own thoughts and actions that we have the capacity to control, and therefore we should be most concerned about them first. During my last few years in the military, I have witnessed example after example of cases where young folks got themselves into some trouble and were punished for it. Interestingly enough, I rarely saw the leadership reevaluate the culture of their organization to see if the young person was simply following the example of those above them. As leaders, we have a responsibility to enforce good order and discipline. We have a responsibility to demonstrate it as well.

This point was really driven home to me during my third assignment at Elmendorf Air Force Base, Alaska. I hadn't been there long and before meeting with one of the Airmen, I was briefed on all his issues, and basically he had been labeled as a problem child. After meeting him, it was clear he had a chip on his shoulder but other than that, he seemed respectful, knowledgeable, and professional. Of course, first impressions can often be wrong. So, I refrained from making a judgment and moved forward. As the months went on, we had experienced a few issues with the Airman but nothing I would consider to be overly disruptive. However, some of the section supervisors felt we should deny the Airman reenlistment and transition him out of the Air Force. I didn't see grounds for such a drastic response and refused to submit the paperwork to the Commander for consideration.

A few months later, the Airman received orders and was reassigned to another unit. As I continued to keep tabs on him, he seemed to have really turned his career around and was doing great. As I started to look at the section he had left, I found that several other Airmen whom had been labeled as problem children and were not doing well. Again, nothing outrageous just minor issues with the supervisor. As I started to dig deeper into the issue, it became clear the issue was the supervisor, not the Airmen. You see, he would say things and do things which were not appropriate in the work place. Seeing this, they would do similar things only to be hammered for it. It was the typical "do as I say not as I do" type scenario. Luckily, when we replaced the supervisor the Airmen all made a full recovery. I only wish I had dug a little deeper into this earlier.

Are you leading by example?

Sometimes BE THE EXAMPLE is simply a matter of reflecting a positive attitude. A couple of years ago, I attended a live webinar called ©Leadercast and one of the speakers was former Navy SEAL Commander, Lieutenant Commander Rorke Denver. During his speech, he shared a lesson he had learned during his initial SEAL training which really drove the point of BE THE EXAMPLE home. In his story, he talks about how during his final training exercise, when they were about midway through, it was obvious they were going to fail. Cleary feeling the pressure, the class leader (the senior ranking officer) is running around the compound like a chicken with his head cut off, screaming out orders.

Because of this, the fevered pitch of the entire group was intolerable, they simply couldn't perform.

Lieutenant Commander Denver then goes on to talk about how this Master Chief Petty Officer comes walking out and calls all the officers over to him. Once all the officers come over, the Master Chief shares with them some advice and a leadership cue (tip) that he had been taught by a Master Chief from Vietnam. He said, "It's never failed and it is the best thing you are ever going to learn in SEAL training." As the officers are sitting there eager to hear what he had to say, the Master Chief said "As leaders, people, at a minimum, are going to mimic your behavior." He went on to share these simple yet critically import words "calm is contagious". Lieutenant Commander Denver goes on to explain how this advice has never been proven wrong and how you can supplement any word for calm and it will still remain true. Panic is contagious. Chaos is contagious. Stupid is 100% contagious.

The point is, and this is something that I myself have found to be true, people will feed off and reflect whatever energy the leader is putting out. I was lucky and discovered this early enough in my career that I believe it was directly responsible for much of my success. It wasn't always easy. In fact, there were days in the morning when it would seem like my son would do whatever he could to get me mad before I headed off to work. However, rather than carry this negative energy into the building with me, I would sit in my car and listen to soft music until I could walk through the door with a smile on my face and my attitude in check.

What type of energy are you putting out when you walk into work?

Another great example of this happened when I was stationed at Kadena Air Base, Japan. I hadn't been on base long and we started to gear up for a training exercise. Wanting to get a good understanding of how the mobility process worked, I went in and had our Unit Deployment Manager bump one of our folks off the deployment roster and plug me in. When I showed up to process through the mobility line, there were no officers in our group and as a Chief and senior enlisted person, I was put in charge. At first everything was normal, hurry up and go from here to there, wait, then hurry up and go from there to somewhere else, wait, and do it again and again. As this went on, it was clear the process was broken and things were not happening as smoothly as they should.

Flash forward to where we are now in our twelfth hour of processing; we hadn't slept or eaten anything all day. We are hanging out in the base theater and all we are waiting on is for someone to come and sign for us. The tension is building in the room and I'm starting to feel like if I don't get something to eat, I may lose my composure. However, understanding that everyone in the room is feeding off the energy I'm putting out, I'm doing all I can to keep it together and keep a smile on my face. Then, finally, I get the notice that the person who could sign for us just pulled into the parking lot. I rush to the door to meet him and I can see this Senior Master Sergeant is visibly pissed off. Knowing that the theater is a tinderbox just waiting to explode into a fire of heated outrage, I pull him off to the side away from the crowd. I then proceed to explain to him, the situation and how I expected him, as a Senior Noncommissioned Officer, to set aside whatever was going on in his head and get himself in check. As it turned out, this particular Senior Master Sergeant was an exceptional Senior Noncommissioned Officer.

He quickly regained his composure and did what he had to in order to get us released back to our units.

Whether you're walking past trash on your way into the building, using inappropriate jokes, putting the coffee pot back empty, or taking extended lunches, know that someone is watching you. More importantly, understand what your people see is what they will believe is ok. Mentorship isn't about what you say. It's about who you are and what you do. Your people are always watching. Acknowledge this and set the example.

Are you the type of leader people want to become?

"Leadership is much more an art, a belief, a condition of the heart, than a set of

things to do. The visible signs of artful leadership are expressed, ultimately, in its practice."

~ Max DePree

BE THE EXAMPLE!

CONCLUSION

"We cannot always build the future for our youth, but we can build our youth for the future."

~ Franklin D. Roosevelt

No one will ever be what he or she is not willing to work to become. Leadership is like most things is life. There is no easy button or secret get good quick formula, and dreaming about it won't do the trick either. Face it, anyone can dream...but it takes commitment, passion, and determination to make a dream come true. There is nothing that can stop a person who remains teachable. Just as, there is nothing that can help a person with a closed mind. To lead, you must continue to learn and grow. Of course, you know this or you wouldn't be reading this book.

As I said in the introduction and throughout this book, I shared with you many stories from different periods of my military career. I share these not to impress you but to impress upon you the impact these basic leadership skills have had on my career and to help illustrate how you may see them materialize in your own organization. Do not let the simplicity of these skills deter you from using them. It is the simplest of actions which can yield the greatest benefits and that is certainly the case here.

Often times in life, there are those once in a lifetime opportunities...the ones that whether we miss them or not, they will change our lives forever. Consider this, the lessons in this book may just be one of those defining moments for you.

Are you willing to apply these lessons and become a leader worth following?

"There are three essentials to leadership: humility, clarity and courage."

~ Fuchan Yuan

CONCLUSION

SPECIAL THANKS!

I would like to say THANK YOU to some special people who really helped me with this book:

Jocelyn Campbell

Paul Gustavson

Lisa Hoffman

Karen Matus

CONCLUSION

ABOUT THE AUTHOR

"When you truly believe in yourself and what you are trying to accomplish, others will believe in you and your vision as well."

~ Mike T. Lightner

Mike Lightner is a retired Chief Master Sergeant from the United States Air Force with extensive knowledge and experience in team leadership and personnel development. In his last position, as the Aircrew Flight Equipment Career Field Manager, he oversaw the leadership, growth, development and management of over 5,200 Total Force (Active Duty, Air National Guard, and Reserve Airmen, and civilian employees) worldwide. Additional, Mike was responsible for the inspection, maintenance, acquisition, and sustainment of over $8 Billion in critical life sustaining aircrew and passenger safety, survival, and chemical defense equipment.

As a John C. Maxwell Certified Coach, Teacher, and Speaker, Mike offers workshops, seminars, keynote speaking, and coaching, aiding your personal and professional growth through study and practical application of proven leadership methods.

Mike's passion is to develop leaders who, in turn, have a passion to develop leaders. If this is the type culture you would like to create within your organization, he stands ready to help you achieve your goal!